International Food Library

FOOD IN
MEXICO

International Food Library

FOOD IN
MEXICO

Paolo Gomez

Rourke Publications, Inc.
Vero Beach, Florida 32964

Library of Congress Cataloging-in-Publication Data

Gomez, Paolo, 1948-
  Food in Mexico/by Paolo Gomez.
    p. cm. - (International food series)
  Includes index.
  Summary: Surveys food products, customs, and preparation in Mexico, describing regional dishes, cooking techniques, and recipes for a variety of meals.
  ISBN 0-86625-341-6
  1. Cookery, Mexican - Juvenile literature. 2. Food habits - Mexico - Juvenile literature. 3. Mexico - Social life and customs - Juvenile literature. [1. Cookery, Mexican. 2. Food habits - Mexico. 3. Mexico - Social life and customs.] I. Title. II. Series.
TX716.M4G66   1989
394. 1'0972-dc19   88-31529
                    CIP
                    AC

CONTENTS

AN INTRODUCTION TO MEXICO

The country of Mexico lies to the south of the United States, and the two countries share a 2,000 mile border that stretches from California to Texas. To the west of Mexico is the Pacific Ocean, and to the east, the Gulf of Mexico. Mexico's neighbors to the south are Guatamala and Belize. This generally mountainous country has a large central plateau of between 3,000 and 6,500 feet high. The Sierra Madre mountain chains to the east and west meet south of the plateau near Mexico's capital, Mexico City. There the volcanic peaks of Popocatepetl and Citlaltepetl rise to heights of around 18,000 feet.

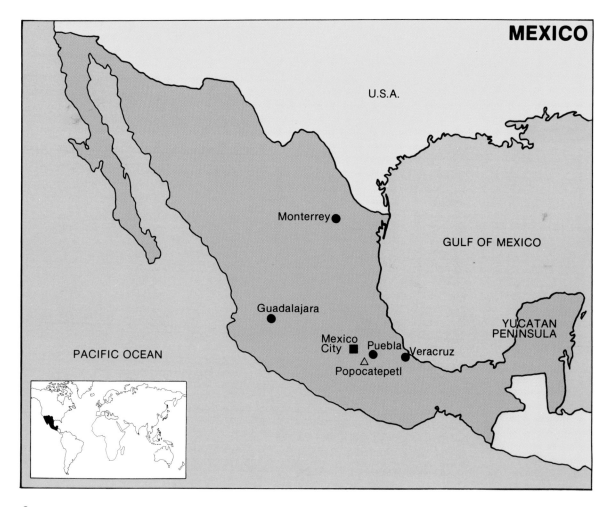

The Mexican people are a blend of Indian and Spanish traits.

Mexico's population is around 80 million and increasing rapidly. Nearly one-third of Mexico's people live in the three main cities, Mexico City, Monterrey, and Guadalajara. Many people who were born in villages are moving to towns and cities in search of work, and overcrowding is a problem in some places.

The population of Mexico is of mixed heritage. Until the early sixteenth century, the country was inhabited exclusively by Indians, including the Mayas and Aztecs. The Indian cultures, rich in ceremony and steeped in tradition, have left a wealth of archaeological sites that are still being explored.

When the Spanish arrived in 1519, they found silver and other precious metals that they needed to finance their wars in Europe. They decided to stay, and for almost three hundred years Mexicans lived under Spanish rule. Mexicans and Spaniards intermarried, and soon most people were of mixed descent. Spanish became the national language, and Christianity the national religion.

Mexico today is a developed industrial nation, with an expanding economy based on minerals, oil and gas, and agriculture.

AGRICULTURE IN MEXICO

Mexico's climate varies from extreme heat to extreme cold, and much of its land is mountainous and dry. Only about half the land in Mexico can be farmed, and only one-eighth can be planted with crops. The non-agricultural areas contain the mountains, urban developments, and forest.

The west coast and the northern plateau regions are exceptionally dry, and nearly all the agricultural land there must be irrigated. Farther south, the rainfall increases, and the land is easier to cultivate. But in the tropical lowlands of the Yucatan Peninsula, the rain brings drainage problems that often result in flooding. This means that to expand the country's farmland, Mexico must either bring more land under irrigation or drain and develop the lowlands. Both options are expensive.

Most Mexican farms are small and unmechanized.

Mexico has a large fishing industry that ranks seventh in the world.

Most Mexican farms are comparatively small. One of the results of the Revolution of 1910 was that the large, privately owned estates were split up into smaller units. Today, privately owned farms or ranches must not have more than 600 acres of grazing land or 300 acres of irrigated land. Some farms, called *ejidos*, owned by the government and operated by a group of villagers or a family unit, are smaller. With an average size of 35 to 40 acres, *ejidos* are too small to mechanize and run efficiently, and the yield per acre remains low.

Even though Mexico has not yet fully developed its agricultural potential, it is the world's sixth largest meat producer and the seventh most important fishing nation. Over twenty of its crops are placed in the top ten of world production, including corn, cotton, tomatoes, avocados, peppers, sugar cane, citrus fruits, and tea. Most of Mexico's agricultural produce is consumed locally.

9

FOOD IN MEXICO

Mexico's food, like its people, is a cheerful blend of Indian and Spanish. The Indian diet consisted of corn, beans, chilies, sweet potatoes, tomatoes, different kinds of squashes, avocados, nuts, vanilla, cocoa, bananas, and other tropical fruits. Meat was limited to wild pig, deer, rabbit, armadillo, and iguana. Those who were lucky enough to live near the coast had a choice of fish and seafood. The Indians invented hundreds of delicious ways to cook their basic ingredients, and many of these recipes survive today.

The *conquistadores* brought with them their favorite foods from Spain. Some of these, like oranges, rice, and spices, had been introduced when Spain was invaded by the Moors from North Africa in the eighth century. The great Spanish galleons also transported wheat, sugar cane, onions, and garlic across the seas to Mexico. Noting that the land was suitable for livestock, they began to raise cattle, pigs, sheep, and goats.

Most Mexicans prefer to shop at markets like this *tiangui*.

Indian markets offer a wide choice of vegetables.

Shopping is a social occasion in Mexico. In the cities, modern supermarkets have sprung up, but most people still prefer to visit the local market to pick up fresh vegetables, herbs, and spices. Out shopping, Mexicans will always stop to chat with their friends and acquaintances. A typical Indian-style market is called a *tiangui*, a name that refers to the canvases used there. One canvas is spread out on the ground to display the vendor's wares, while the other is hoisted up overhead as protection against sun and rain.

CORN

Corn, also known as maize, is an important crop all over the world, ranking second only to wheat. In Mexico, it is the most important food crop, occupying half of the total cultivated land area. The principal growing regions are in central and southern Mexico.

The word *maize* comes from the old Indian word *ma-hiz*. Corn originated in the Americas and has been the basis of the Mexican diet for thousands of years. Archaeologists believe that corn was eaten by cave dwellers in southern Mexico as long ago as 5,000 B.C. The great ancient Indian civilizations of Mexico thrived on it.

Fresh ears of corn are sold by roadside vendors.

Corn is Mexico's most important crop.

Although corn production has improved in recent years, Mexico still cannot grow enough to feed the country's rapidly growing population and has to import some from abroad. One reason for this is that corn is grown mostly by small farmers on land that is not irrigated. Most of the very small farmers are pleased if they are able to grow enough corn to feed their family. They rarely have any surplus to sell. Only 15 percent of Mexico's corn crop is grown on irrigated land by land-owning farmers who have large enough farms and the financial incentives to employ modern farming techniques.

In the towns, people are beginning to eat more meat, vegetables, and fruit, and less corn, but in the poorer rural areas corn is still very much the staple. It is usually ground into flour, *masa harina*, and mixed with water to make tortillas. Tortillas are turned into many dishes like enchiladas, quesadillas, tostados, burritos, tacos, and totopos.

SUGAR CANE

Sugar cane is grown in many parts of the world today, and it is interesting to see how this crop came to Mexico from its original home on the island of New Guinea in Southeast Asia. Traveling west with the ancient trade routes, it came under cultivation in India and is mentioned in historical records dating back to the fourth century B.C. Sugar cane reached the Middle East and North Africa via Persia (now Iran), with which India had close links, and was in turn introduced to Spain and southern Europe by the conquering Moors from Africa.

When Hernan Cortès and his men invaded Mexico in the early sixteenth century, they found that the local Indians did not use any form of sweetening. Sugar cane was unknown, and honey was strictly reserved for the royal courts. Finding the southern plains suitable for cultivating sugar cane, the Spanish imported the crop from Spain and planted it. Today Mexico is one of the world's largest producers of sugar cane and is able to supply enough to satisfy local demand.

Harvesting sugar cane by hand is a long and tiring job.

Sugar cane was introduced to Mexico by the Spanish settlers.

Most of Mexico's sugar cane is grown in the state of Veracruz, where the government plans to expand agriculture. Lying on the western fringe of the Gulf of Mexico, Veracruz is also important for its production of oranges, lemons, mangoes, bananas, and other fruit.

Sugar cane is harvested once a year. The harvest is a long and tiring time for the agricultural workers. Since the previous year, when the plants were cut down, the canes have grown back to their full height of 10 to 20 feet. The stems now measure 1½ to 2 inches in diameter. These tall, strong canes now have to be cut by hand and bundled onto trucks that take them off for processing into sugar granules.

REGIONAL COOKING

Certain foods such as tortillas, tomatoes, onions, garlic, and chilies, are used for cooking throughout Mexico, but many towns also have their own special recipes. Some have even become famous. These dishes are usually based on local ingredients that are considered the best of their kind. Others may be attributed to a certain type of cooking that has been invented or perfected in the town.

The town of Puebla, 80 miles southeast of Mexico City and nestled high in the rugged mountains, is often referred to as Mexico's gastronomic center. Puebla's cuisine was influenced by the French when, during another turbulent episode in Mexico's history, they held the town as part of their territory under the control of the Emperor Maximilian. Puebla has become famous for its *mole Poblana*, a savory chocolate sauce derived from an old Indian recipe that is served with chicken or turkey.

Most of Mexico's beef is produced in the northern states of Sonara, Chihuahua, Coahuila, and Nuevo Leon. High in the eastern Sierra Madre mountains, Monterrey is renowned for its excellent beef and goat meat. Traditionally, food in this area is heavy and very filling. The ranch workers need three hearty meals each day, probably beginning with *huevos rancheros*, or ranch-style eggs, that are served with beans, avocado, and tortillas.

Fish and seafood have always played an important part in the Mexican diet. Montezuma, the Aztec Emperor, used to have fresh fish brought to his court in what is now Mexico City by runners from the seaport of Veracruz. Both the Pacific and Gulf waters are rich in seafood. The Gulf of California has wonderful oysters and abalone, while the gentle east coast waters provide many kinds of fish, crabs, lobster, and shrimp.

Mexico's coastal waters are rich in fis and seafood.

MEXICAN FESTIVALS

Mexican festivals are a swirl of color and gaiety. Each village celebrates the anniversary of at least one patron saint. It may be the saint for whom the village or church was named or a saint who is said to have visited the village long ago. Whatever the reason, everyone puts on their best clothes and flocks to the main square where they dance, sing, and have fun long into the night. Even the children, the little girls in their frills and ribbons and the boys excited and mischievous, stay on until the cafe owners reluctantly begin to pack up and the weary band ceases to play. Sometimes the festivals can last for three days and nights — and the Mexicans enjoy every minute of it!

Christmas is the longest holiday in the Mexican calendar. The festivities begin on December 16 and last through Epiphany, or Twelfth Night, on January 6. Among the celebrations, Christmas Day and Epiphany are the special family occasions. On these days the whole family, which is usually large, will get together to celebrate.

Mexican musicians are always on hand for a fiesta.

Dressed in traditional costumes, Mexicans enjoy singing and dancing.

National holidays in Mexico also include two state celebrations. September 16 is Independence Day, which commemorates the overthrow of Spanish colonial rule in 1810. May 5 celebrates the anniversary of the victorious Battle of Puebla, when the Mexicans defeated the invading French forces of Napoleon III. It was only a temporary halt to the French advance, and Mexico later came under the control of the European Emperor Maximilian for a period of three years before the French were eventually driven out. These holidays appeal to the Mexicans' patriotic pride, and dishes in the colors of the Mexican flag (green, white, and red) are traditionally served.

A BANQUET MENU FOR A FESTIVE OCCASION

Guacamole With Corn Chips
Bean Soup
Peppers Stuffed With Shrimp
Estofado
Pineapple Sorbet

Each course in this meal should be served separately, with a slight pause between courses to aid digestion. The recipes are designed to feed six people.

Guacamole

    3 large ripe avocados
    1 onion, finely chopped
    2 chilies with seeds removed, finely chopped
    2 teaspoons minced garlic
    2 teaspoons lemon juice
    1 teaspoon olive oil

1. Peel avocados and remove pits from center. Mash avocados until no large pieces are left.
2. Add other ingredients and mix well. Serve as a dip with corn chips.

Bean Soup

    1 can red kidney or black beans, drained
    5 cups water
    ¼ lb. salt pork, diced
    1 onion, chopped
    ½ sweet red pepper, seeded and chopped
    1 chili, seeded and finely chopped
    1 teaspoon minced garlic
    1 teaspoon oregano
    1 tablespoon oil

1. Heat the oil in a pan and gently fry the onion, garlic, sweet pepper, chili, oregano, and pork for 5 minutes.
2. Add the water and beans. Cover and simmer for 20 minutes. Serve hot.

Guacamole with corn chips.

Peppers Stuffed With Shrimp

    6 Anaheim peppers, seeded
    1 onion, finely chopped
    3 tomatoes, chopped
    1 cup cooked shelled shrimp
    1 cup cooked rice
    1 teaspoon minced garlic
    1 teaspoon fresh coriander, finely chopped
    1 tablespoon oil

1. Heat the oil in a pan and gently fry the onion and garlic.
2. Preheat the oven to 350 degrees.
3. Add the tomatoes, rice, shrimp, and coriander to the pan and mix together. Remove from heat.
4. Stuff each of the peppers with the mixture. Place in the oven and cook for 20 minutes. Serve hot.

Estofado

    2 lbs. flank steak, cut into 1-inch cubes
    2 onions, chopped
    1 sweet green pepper, seeded and chopped
    6 medium potatoes, peeled and halved
    1 can tomatoes, chopped
    1 cup beef stock
    1 teaspoon minced garlic
    1 teaspoon salt
    1 teaspoon mustard seed
    2 teaspoons chili powder
    1 teaspoon oregano
    1 bay leaf
      black pepper to taste
    2 tablespoons oil

1. Heat the oil in a large pan and gently fry the onions, garlic, and oregano for 2 minutes. Add the meat and fry for 5 more minutes, then add the bell pepper and fry for 1 more minute.
2. Add the tomatoes, beef stock, black pepper, mustard, chili powder, and bay leaf and bring to a boil. Cover and simmer for 30 minutes.
3. Add the potatoes. Continue to simmer for 30 minutes more. Serve hot.

Pineapple Sorbet

    1 cup water
    ½ cup sugar
    1 cup chopped pineapple, fresh or canned
    1 teaspoon lemon juice
    2 egg whites

1. Place the sugar and water in a pan and heat on low or medium until the sugar dissolves. Remove from the heat and allow to cool.
2. Put the pineapple through a blender to make a pulpy sauce. Add this sauce to the cooled sugar syrup, and then add enough water to make the mixture 2½ cups.

Try freezing your sorbet in a hollowed-out pineapple.

3. Pour the mixture into a container and leave in the freezer until nearly firm.

4. Whisk the egg whites until they are stiff. Then using a wooden spoon, work them into the pineapple mixture.

5. Pour the sorbet into six small freezer-proof dessert bowls and freeze. Serve straight from the freezer.

AN EAST COAST MEAL

Tortillas With Mexican Sauce
Veracruz-Style Fish
Rice
Fresh Papaya

This menu is typical of a seafood meal served on a balmy evening in one of the many tiny ports on Mexico's Gulf coast. Serve the tortillas with Mexican sauce before the rest of the meal and end with a dessert of fresh papaya. If you don't find papaya at your supermarket, serve any fresh fruit in season — strawberries, peaches, or pineapple, for instance.

Veracruz-Style Fish.

Mexican Sauce

  1 small onion
  6 tomatoes
  2 chilies with seeds taken out
  1 teaspoon minced garlic
  1 teaspoon fresh coriander, finely chopped
  2 teaspoons olive oil
  1 teaspoon wine vinegar

1. Finely chop the onion, tomatoes, and chilis. Mix in a bowl with the other ingredients, and serve with tortillas.

Veracruz-Style Fish

  4 fish fillets (snapper, halibut or sole)
    juice of 1 lemon
  1 onion, chopped
  ½ sweet red pepper, seeded and chopped
  2 chilies, seeded and finely chopped
  1 can tomatoes, chopped
  1 tablespoon capers
 12 pitted olives
  ½ teaspoon oregano
  1 bay leaf
  1 teaspoon minced garlic
  1 teaspoon salt
  1 tablespoon oil

1. Place the fish fillets in a casserole dish and squeeze lemon juice over them.
2. Preheat oven to 350 degrees.
3. Heat the oil in a pan and gently fry the onion, garlic, sweet pepper, chili, and oregano for 3 minutes.
4. Add the tomatoes, salt, bay leaf, olives and capers and cook for 15 minutes. Remove from the heat and pour over the fish fillets.
5. Place in the oven and cook for 20 minutes. Serve hot, garnished with lemon wedges and rice.

A MEAL FROM PUEBLA

Apple Soup
Chicken With Mole Sauce
Rice Or Tortillas

A full Mexican meal would normally consist of six or
seven courses, but this shortened menu will be plenty
for four for lunch or dinner. The soup should be served
first, followed by the chicken and rice or tortillas.

**A Mexican woman
making tortillas.**

Apple Soup

> 2 apples, peeled and chopped into ¼-inch cubes
> ½ onion, finely chopped
> ½ cup tomato juice
> 4 cups chicken stock
> 1 tablespoon fresh coriander, finely chopped
> 2 tablespoons apple juice
> 1 tablespoon butter

1. Heat the butter in a pan and gently fry the
   onion for 2 minutes.
2. Add the tomato juice, bring to a boil, and
   simmer for 3 minutes.
3. Add the chicken stock and apple juice, and
   simmer for 10 minutes.
4. Add the cubed apple, simmer for 1 minute so
   that the apple is hot but still hard. Serve
   garnished with coriander.

Chicken With Mole Sauce

4 hot cooked chicken breasts
1 sweet green pepper, seeded and
  finely chopped
4 chili peppers, seeded and finely chopped
1 onion, finely chopped
1 lb. tomatoes, quartered
2 tablespoons oil
1 tablespoon flaked almonds
1 tablespoon unsalted peanuts
1 tablespoon raisins
1 tablespoon sesame seeds
1 teaspoon minced garlic
1 teaspoon cinnamon powder
1 teaspoon fennel seeds
1 teaspoon salt
2 cloves
  black pepper, to taste
1 tortilla, shredded, or
½ cup fresh breadcrumbs
3 squares cooking chocolate
4 cups cooked rice

1. Heat the oil in a large pan and fry the onion, garlic, sweet pepper, and chili for 3 minutes. Add the tomatoes, almonds, raisins, peanuts, sesame seeds, fennel seeds, and cloves, and cook for 5 minutes. Remove from the heat and let cool.
2. When cooled, put the contents of the pan in a blender and mix until you have a thick sauce.
3. Return the sauce to the pan. Add the cinnamon, salt, chicken stock, and tortilla or breadcrumbs, and bring the mixture to a boil. Add the chocolate and stir the mixture until the chocolate melts.
4. Pour the sauce over the hot chicken and serve hot with boiled rice.

AN EVERYDAY MEAL

In between the main meals of the day Mexicans love to eat little snacks made using corn tortillas, like tacos, enchiladas, and burritos. The following recipe would make enough for a lunch for four people.

Mexican snacks.

Chicken Enchiladas

> 12 7-inch corn tortillas
> 2 cups olive oil
> 3 cooked chicken breasts, skinned and boned
> 1 onion, finely chopped
> 1 jalapeno pepper, finely chopped
> 6 tablespoons sour cream
> 2 cups grated Cheddar cheese

1. Heat the olive oil in a large pan. Using tongs, pick up a tortilla and dip it into the hot fat to soften it. Repeat this for the remaining 11 tortillas. Lay the tortillas on a large board.
2. To make the filling, first shred the chicken breasts. Then mix together the onion, jalapeño pepper, and sour cream in a bowl. Preheat the oven to 350 degrees.
5. Put a small amount of the shredded chicken lengthwise across the center of each tortilla. Add a spoonful of the sour cream mixture and roll each tortilla tightly. Place the enchiladas in a greased casserole dish, sprinkle with cheese, and bake in the oven for 15 to 20 minutes. Serve hot onto warmed plates with side dishes of guacamole (for recipe see Chapter 11) and Mexican sauce (for recipe see Chapter 9).

GLOSSARY OF COOKING TERMS

For those readers who are less experienced in the kitchen, the following list explains the cooking terms used in this book.

Blender	A piece of kitchen equipment used to mix ingredients together
Boned	Having had the bones removed
Chopped	Cut into small pieces measuring about ½ inch
Finely chopped	Cut into very small pieces measuring about ⅛ inch
Garnished	Decorated
Minced	Chopped into tiny pieces or put through a mincer
Preheat	Heat beforehand to the required temperature
Seeded	Having had the seeds removed
Shelled	Having had the shells removed
Shredded	Cut into lengths of 1-2 inches, about ¼ inch across
Simmer	Cook on top of the stove at a low temperature; stoves usually have a setting for simmer
Skinned	Having had the skin removed
Spoon measurements	Tablespoons and teaspoons should be filled only to the level of the spoon's edge, not heaped.
Whisk	To beat using a hand whisk or electric mixer

MEXICAN COOKING

For the recipes in this book you will need the following special ingredients:

Capers Small green buds or berries sold in jars at most supermarkets.

Chilies and peppers Mexicans use many different kinds of chilies and peppers. The recipes in this book use small, hot chilies, Anaheim peppers, red and green sweet peppers, and jalapeño peppers. These can all be bought in large supermarkets. Jalapeño peppers are usually sold in cans.

Herbs Bay leaves, coriander, and oregano are needed for these recipes. If possible, buy them fresh from a farmers' market or in the produce section of your supermarket. Otherwise, substitute dried herbs.

Masa harina This corn flour can be found in most supermarkets and health food stores.

Oil Olive oil and peanut oil are the best kinds of oil to use in Mexican cooking. Olive oil is cholesterol-free and should be used when serving guests on a low cholesterol diet.

Olives Black or green olives come in cans and jars and are carried by all supermarkets.

Spices Chili powder, cinammon powder, fennel seeds, mustard seeds, and sesame seeds can all be found in the spice section of your local supermarket.

Tortillas Sold in the dairy case of most supermarkets.

Tortillas, cooked on a griddle, are a staple food in Mexico.

INDEX

We would like to thank and acknowledge the following people for the use of their photographs and transparencies:

Anthony Blake Ltd: 21, 23, 24; Bruce Coleman Ltd: Michael Klinec, 17; (M A L Fogden): T/Page; (Melinda Berge): 7; Mexican Ministry of Tourism: Cover; Pictures Color Library: Cover, 28; Sean Sprague/Mexicolore: 8/9, 10/11, 12 12/13, 14/15, 18, 19.